SOCIAL MEDIA CAREER BUILDING™

20 GREAT
CAREER-BUILDING
ACTIVITIES USING
FACEBOOK®

CATHLEEN SMALL

ROSEN
PUBLISHING®

New York

Published in 2017 by The Rosen Publishing Group, Inc.
29 East 21st Street, New York, NY 10010

First Edition

Library of Congress Cataloging-in-Publication Data

Names: Small, Cathleen, author.
Title: 20 great career-building activities using Facebook /
Cathleen Small.
Other titles: Twenty great career-building activities using Face-
book
Description: New York : Rosen Publishing, 2017. | Series:
Social media career building | Audience: Grades 7–12. | In-
cludes bibliographical references and index.
Identifiers: LCCN 2016021380 | ISBN 9781508172628 (library
bound)
Subjects: LCSH: Facebook (Firm)—Juvenile literature. | Busi-
ness networks—Juvenile literature. | Employment portfolios—
Juvenile literature. | Career development—Juvenile literature.
Classification: LCC HM743.F33 S63 2017 | DDC 650.1—dc23
LC record available at https://lccn.loc.gov/2016021380

Manufactured in China

CONTENTS

INTRODUCTION

Back in the day, when you wanted to create a résumé, you did it on paper. A résumé was printed on good quality paper and mailed to prospective employers or admissions counselors. Your portfolio was a physical object that you mailed or presented to employers and admissions departments as well—a folder containing what represented your best work. You carried it with you when you went to any sort of interview, and you carefully laid out your work for the interviewer to see.

Things have gotten much simpler now. All of this can be done electronically. Portfolio items can be scanned and saved as image files (such as JPEGs) or portable document format (PDF) files. You can then email them out or post them to a website. Even easier, social media can be used to create a dynamic, easily updatable résumé and portfolio. You can even make a professional Facebook page to show potential employers or admissions counselors the latest and greatest content in your portfolio and your most up-to-date résumé.

It really couldn't be simpler. So what are you waiting for?

By the time you get to the interview, you will most likely have already shared all of your relevant experience and portfolio items with the interviewer electronically.

CHAPTER ONE

The Scoop on Facebook

Unless you don't use the internet or know anybody else who does, you undoubtedly have heard of Facebook. Even if you haven't used it much, it's everywhere in our social culture. The little blue and gray thumbs-up "Like" symbol is a familiar logo that appears all over the Internet. The Facebook logo appears on all manner of business webpages as a means of marketing for the company: "Share us on Facebook!"

MARK ZUCKERBERG: THE FATHER OF FACEBOOK

The users and purpose of Facebook have changed over the past decade, but fundamentally it remains the same groundbreaking social media site that Mark Zuckerberg designed when he was a student at Harvard University.

As a student at Harvard, Zuckerberg's original goal was to create a central website where Harvard students could connect with each other. Amazingly, it took Zuckerberg only ten days to write the code for the site. And it was immediately popular among Harvard students when it went live in February 2004, boasting more than a thousand registered users within the first twenty-four hours.

Facebook soon expanded to other universities, and in 2006 it was opened to anyone over the age of thirteen. By 2008, Facebook had one hundred million active registered users, and now more than a billion people use Facebook every day. The site's reach is nothing short of staggering.

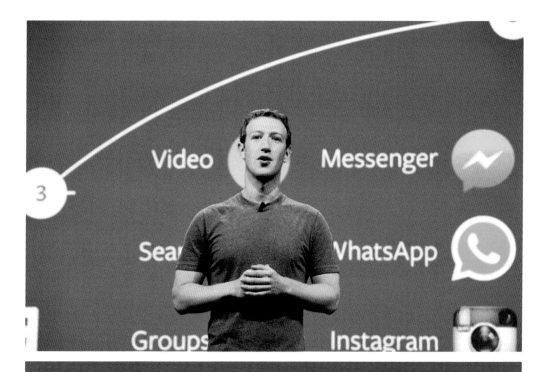

Mark Zuckerberg, the face behind social media giant Facebook, which has changed the way we connect with people online.

WHO'S USING FACEBOOK

So who *are* these more than one billion users? Well, for starters, many are people who use it for personal connections—to socialize and keep in touch with family and friends. Facebook gives people a place to post pictures of their kids, their significant others, their pets, or even themselves, as well as a place to share their thoughts, their feelings on current issues, their joys, and their sorrows. It's a place where anything goes— except inappropriate content. That can be a blessing and a curse, as we'll discuss in more detail later. People who use Facebook for personal reasons are often looking to keep in touch with people or to make new connections with new potential friends with similar interests. It's a whole virtual world of potential friends right at your fingertips.

Many people use Facebook as a business tool as well. They may or may not use it for personal communication, too, but, regardless, they use it as a platform to maintain and grow their business. Users can create specific pages for their business, to keep the business a separate entity from their personal page, and they can then invite friends to "Like" their business page so that posts from the business will show up in their News Feeds later on. It is, essentially, an elaborate marketing tool for businesses.

Along similar lines, some people may choose to use Facebook as a professional tool. Similar to creating a page for a business, users can create a page to act as a sort of virtual résumé or portfolio. This allows users to keep their professional and career-focused posts on the page that acts as a résumé or portfolio, separate from their personal page. And just as a user might ask friends to Like a business page on Facebook, a user could also ask friends to Like a portfolio or résumé page, so that new posts about professional developments will show up on friends' News Feeds.

 BEYOND FACEBOOK

Facebook is currently the most widely used social media platform, but it is far from the only one. According to a Pew Research Center 2015 study, 72 percent of adults who use the internet use Facebook, while Instagram, LinkedIn, and Twitter run far behind, with adult internet user percentages of 28, 25, and 23 percent, respectively. Still, if you're looking for the widest reach possible, it makes sense to extend your reach beyond Facebook. Instagram is primarily a photo-sharing social media site, so it can be useful if you can use images to support your professional profile. LinkedIn is designed specifically for career building and networking, so it's highly advisable to set up a profile on that platform. And Twitter is used for broadcasting short messages of 140 characters or fewer. If you have short, useful things to say that will enhance your professional profile, Twitter might be a good platform to explore. Twitter also allows for easy cross-posting, so if you post a short message on Twitter, you can have it posted to Facebook simultaneously, saving you a bit of time in your networking efforts.

HOW IT ALL FITS TOGETHER: THE COMPONENTS OF FACEBOOK

If you're not already an experienced Facebook user, you might be wondering how all of this fits together. Basically, it breaks down into three pieces: profiles, pages, and groups.

Your Facebook profile photo can say volumes about you. Do you want to come across as fun and free-spirited or as poised and professional?

THE PROFILE

The heart of your Facebook presence is your profile. It is the place where you will likely make your personal posts—posting pictures of friends or family, posting your general thoughts about life and what you're up to, commenting on friends' posts, and so on. That is, if you choose to use Facebook for socializing. If you want to use Facebook solely as a professional tool, you probably won't use your profile all that much. You'll have to establish it, because you can't have a Facebook presence *without* a profile, but you'll probably find you don't use it for much.

THE PAGE

The second piece is a page. As mentioned, you can create a Facebook page for your business or as a sort of résumé or portfolio to showcase your experience and achievements. The page will be linked to your profile, but it will be separate from it in that people can Like your page without actually being your Facebook friend. When they do that, they will get posts from your page, but they won't see any of your personal posts from your personal profile in their News Feeds. But keep in mind, it's pretty easy to track back to a personal profile from a page and, depending on your privacy settings, your personal profile might be visible. So even if you are creating a

People can look at your Facebook profile or page on their computer or on a smartphone.

page for your professional life, it's wise to keep your personal profile clean and free of anything that might embarrass you professionally.

GROUPS

The third piece of the puzzle is groups. You can create groups on Facebook and invite people to them. When you do, anyone who is part of your Facebook group will get all of the posts you make in that group—as well as all of the posts other members make in it. But you can also use groups a bit differently—you might not create a group on your own, but simply join other preexisting groups and use them to network with people to drive interest in your professional page. For example, maybe you're launching a furniture-painting business, but you don't particularly want to create a Facebook group to promote it. You could join a preexisting Facebook group devoted to that topic and simply promote your page and business in it, as long as this follows the guidelines of the group.

LOOKING AHEAD

Facebook might seem temporary and editable, but nothing on the Internet is *truly* temporary. It's important to understand how posting on Facebook works and what it means in terms of considering the content you post. To understand how to control who sees your posts, and what you can control, it's good to have an understanding of privacy settings before you start posting.

CHAPTER TWO

The Internet Is Forever

O n the surface, Facebook looks very flexible. If you post something and later decide you don't want to share that content, you can just delete it, right? In reality, everything on the Internet is permanent in some way—even if you delete it.

You might think you're deleting some-thing, but if it's on the Internet, it's generally there permanently in some way, shape, or form.

WHAT'S IN A POST

Let's start by examining what makes up a Face-book post. Facebook allows you to post several types of content. There are really three main types of posts (and a few others that aren't used very often, so we won't mention them here): text, images, and links.

You can post text, and unlike Twitter, which limits you to 140 characters, you can post as much text as you'd like. Be careful of posts that are text heavy, though. There's no guarantee people will read it if you get too wordy. You can also post images and videos, and you can even combine an image or video with text that describes it. Finally, you can post links to outside content. The how-to on this is very simple—even if you haven't ever used Facebook before, you'll find it's a simple matter of clicking and typing. It takes all of thirty seconds—or maybe a couple of minutes if you're typing a particularly long post.

THE IMPORTANCE OF APPROPRIATE CONTENT

Because it's so effortless to post on Facebook, it can also be easy to post something in the heat of the moment—which is not always the best idea. For example, perhaps your boss reprimanded you at work, and you're frustrated because you think your boss was out of line. So in the heat of the moment, you fire off a quick Facebook post about how angry you are. Maybe it makes you feel better to post it and to see the supportive comments your friends make about how you were wronged, but take a moment to think about the bigger picture.

Your boss might see your post. Or someone who knows your boss might see your post. Either way, your boss might get wind of the fact that you vented your frustration on Facebook, and that could earn you a worse reprimand—or even cost you your job.

"But no one who knows my boss is my Facebook friend!" you might say. "And my posts are set to Friends Only, so my boss won't ever get wind of it!"

Maybe not, but are you really willing to risk it? If it's on Facebook, it *can* be seen. What if one of your friends thinks it's a funny post, so he takes a screenshot of it and shares it on his profile? And someone connected to him on Facebook knows your boss? Or, what if your privacy settings aren't as ironclad as you think they are? Facebook is notorious for tweaking privacy settings, and users don't always find out right away, which means their privacy isn't quite as secure as they thought.

Make sure whatever you post is something you're comfortable with people seeing. You don't want to regret a post later on.

Or maybe your boss really never *does* see the post. What about other people in positions of authority? What about your teachers, or potential future employers? Academic recruiters when you're looking into colleges? A post ranting about how your boss wronged you could be a *major* red flag to future employers or to academic recruiters. They could see it as you refusing to accept blame for your own actions as an employee. Even if you truly *were* wronged, they might still see it as proof that you don't take the time to calm down and think through the consequences of something before reacting.

The same holds true for content that's inappropriate in other ways. Facebook is not the place for sexually suggestive content, for example. It's also not the place to post pictures of a wild party you attended that might call into question your behavior or judgment. Be careful posting links to articles and content that you didn't write—you might think a crude article is funny, but stop and consider whether *everyone* will appreciate it before you post it. Potential employers or academic recruiters are likely to not see the humor in it.

The best plan is to take a moment to consider any content you're going to post: How does it reflect on you? Would it make a potential employer or academic recruiter question your judgment or behavior? If so, it's best not to post it.

WHAT YOU CAN CONTROL

You do have some control over your Facebook profile. You can make thoughtful decisions about the type of

OOPS! FACEBOOK REGRET

According to an ABC News article, nearly one in five social media users in America has regretted something they have posted online. And sometimes, the effects of a hasty post can be devastating. Justin Carter, a teenager from Texas, ended up in jail after he posted a Facebook message that he was going to "shoot up a kindergarten." He was arrested and indicted for making a terrorist threat, even though he had posted "JK" (for "just kidding") with the message and it was made in a trash-talking conversation with some fellow gamers. Understandably, the authorities took it seriously, even though the teen expressed regret for the post and said it was a joke. While in jail, he was seriously beaten.

Obviously, most cases of social media regret don't have *quite* these consequences, but it's something to be aware of. While the consequences of most posts aren't as serious, even embarrassing your family and yourself is best avoided when possible.

content you post. And to a large extent, you can control your privacy settings. Facebook does allow you to customize your privacy for different types of posts: You can make them visible to everyone, to only people in your Friends list, to people in your friends' Friends lists, or to only specific people you select. However, those privacy settings aren't 100 percent infallible. As mentioned before, Facebook sometimes changes how the privacy settings work. That may result in your account not being quite as secure as you intended. The privacy settings are fairly complex, so you might inadvertently set something in a way you hadn't necessarily meant to. But despite this control, there are also some areas where you do *not* have control.

WHAT YOU CANNOT CONTROL

Facebook has a feature called tagging, which allows people to tag you in one of their posts. It might be a picture you're in, or it might just be a text or link post. Regardless, they can tag you if they choose. In the case of images, Facebook has facial-recognition features that will sometimes automatically tag you, even if the original poster didn't manually tag you.

When you're tagged in a post of any type, it means all of your Facebook friends can also see that post. You can imagine how this might become problematic. Suppose there's a picture of you at a party with your arm around someone who is *not* your boyfriend, and you get tagged in the image. Your boyfriend is likely your Facebook friend, and the moment you get tagged, that image will be visible to him. Even if the image was perfectly innocent, you can imagine how it might cause issues with your significant other!

Likewise, if you get tagged in a post about a weekend of partying, your Facebook friends will then get wind of it—and that may not be something you want a potential future employer or academic recruiter seeing.

Another thing you can't control is people sharing your posts. If you post something on Facebook, it *can* be shared by your Facebook friends. Depending on how you've set the privacy for the post, that might not be an issue—if you have set the privacy to Friends Only, then even if your friend shares your post, the only people who will be able to see it are people on *your* Friends list. But if your privacy settings aren't ironclad, the friends of whoever shares your post might be able to see it as well.

And even if you have your privacy set such that only *your* friends can see a post, that doesn't stop one of

Perhaps not the photo you want potential employers or academic recruiters to see!

your friends from taking a screen capture of the post and posting it to their own page as an image. And if that happens, you have absolutely zero control over it.

LOOKING AHEAD

The moral of the story is that once you've posted something on Facebook, you can never be *absolutely certain* that it won't find its way to someplace you might not want it to appear. So it's best to very carefully consider your posts before making them.

Now that you know the importance of careful posting, it's time to consider the root unit of Facebook: your profile.

CHAPTER THREE

What Is a Profile?

A profile is the most basic unit of Facebook. If you have a Facebook account, you have a profile. The amount of information you choose to make public on your profile is up to you, but you must have a basic profile. Having a profile allows you to post content, Like the content posted by other people, and share content. And because you want to use Facebook to further your academic or professional career, it makes sense to put information in your profile that will show you in a positive, professional light.

WHAT GOES INTO A PROFILE?

The Facebook profile section comprises several sections: Work and

The first step to using Facebook is setting up your profile.

Education, Places You've Lived, Contact and Basic Info, Family and Relationships, Details About You, and Life Events. A few fields are mandatory, but most of them are optional. You can choose how much and what

LIKES, FOLLOWS, AND SHARES: HOW THEY REFLECT ON YOU

Once you have a Facebook profile, you can begin to Like your Facebook friends' posts. You can also follow people or businesses on Facebook and share posts that you like from other people. How does that reflect on you?

Any time you Like a post, the audience for that post can see that you Liked it. For example, if you Liked your friend's post about chinchillas, your friend's Aunt Mabel, who is on Facebook, will be able to see that you Liked the post—even if you aren't Facebook friends with Aunt Mabel. This is OK as long as you're fine with people knowing about your love of chinchilla posts, but it might not be so fine if you Like a post with questionable content. If the questionable post is set to Public, that means everyone in the Facebook world will be able to see that you Liked it—and that may not be something you want to do. The same holds true for pages you follow. If the page is a public one, then anyone will be able to see that you follow it.

When you share a post, the only people who can see it are those you choose to share it with—this may be Public, or it might be just people in your Friends list, or Friends of Friends. But do take a moment to think about how something you share reflects on you before you do it. As mentioned earlier, if a post is potentially rude or offensive, it's probably not something you want to share.

you want to add. Your Facebook profile will also include a profile picture and a cover photo. Once you've signed up for Facebook and gone to the News Feed, you'll be able to click Edit Profile on the upper-left portion of the screen to access all of your profile information.

CHOOSE YOUR PROFILE AND COVER PICTURES

The first step in setting up a profile is choosing a profile picture and a cover photo. Your blank profile will show spaces for the profile picture and cover photo,

If you want to post a picture that includes people other than you, make sure they're okay with having their picture posted.

and you can click on the camera icon to upload a picture. Facebook offers some basic cropping tools if you need them, but otherwise the process is pretty straightforward.

One thing to note is that regardless of how you adjust your privacy settings, your profile and cover photos are always public. So be sure to choose images that you're comfortable with everyone in the Facebook world seeing—not just your Facebook friends. For example, some parents aren't comfortable with their children's pictures being seen by the entire world, so they will purposely keep images that include their children out of their profile and cover photos. Children likely aren't an issue for you, but if there is anyone with you in the photo, ask yourself if that other person will be comfortable with having their picture public.

 ## LIST YOUR WORK AND EDUCATION

This section is essentially the basis of your online résumé. Here, you can list schools you've attended, places you've worked, skills you've learned, and so on.

If you click Add a Workplace, you can search for companies in a list that pops up. Facebook has a lot of employers to choose from. But if you've worked for a company that isn't listed, you can also just manually enter the details, including where the company was, what position you held, and how long you worked there. The same holds true for colleges and high schools you've attended.

Don't forget to add your professional skills. If you are using Facebook as an online résumé tool, your potential employers will likely want to see what professional skills you've gained in your education and in your previous employment.

DOCUMENT PLACES YOU'VE LIVED AND BASIC CONTACT INFORMATION

A Facebook profile will allow you to add your hometown, the place you live currently, and any other places you've lived. When you add a place, you'll be able to search for the city from a comprehensive list. If you can't find the city, you can manually add it.

Facebook allows you to enter specific details about the places you've lived, including dates and the exact address. Be very cautious about adding an exact address. In most cases, it is best to keep that information off Facebook. Unfortunately, cyber predators are a real threat, and you don't want to inadvertently give one your home, school, or work address. To be safe, you can even avoid listing your exact city—some people simply enter a region instead of a specific city.

Keep in mind that same security when you're populating the Contact and Basic Info pag academic recruiter e. Facebook allows you to include contact information such as your phone number, email accounts, websites, and address. Think long and hard about what information you want to include there—chances are, you don't want to include your exact address, and even entering your phone number is questionable. Most cell phones now are equipped with GPS tracking capabilities, and it wouldn't be unheard of for a cyber predator to use your cell phone number to track your location.

If you're using Facebook as a professional tool, though, you want to give prospective employers a way to contact you. They can do so through Facebook messaging, but you may also want to include an email address. You still have some worry about cyber predators emailing you and trying to engage you inappropriately, but the danger isn't quite as high—you can always disable your email address. Just be sure to always use caution when responding to people you don't know who email or message you. Don't share any personal information unless you're absolutely certain the person is a legitimate and trustworthy individual.

Your Contact and Basic Info page also includes fields for your birth date and year, your gender, your religious and political views, the languages you speak, and even who you're interested in. All of that information is optional, so fill it out as you desire.

SHARE FAMILY AND RELATIONSHIPS AND DETAILS ABOUT YOU

On the Family and Relationships page, you can include who you're in a relationship with, as well as any family members. If the person is on Facebook, you can link to their profile. If they're not, you can simply list their name and relationship to you.

You can share details about your family on the Family and Relationships page.

On the Details About You page, you can write a little blurb introducing yourself, and you can add in your name pronunciation, any nicknames you go by, and even your favorite quotes.

 ## UPDATE LIFE EVENTS

If you're using Facebook as a professional tool, you may want to list some life events, such as graduating from high school or college, getting new jobs, getting books or papers published, doing military service or volunteer work, or any of a number of other things. The

Life Events page of your profile will walk you through adding life events related to work, education, family, home life, health and wellness, and travel.

LOOKING AHEAD

Your profile is now set, but perhaps you want to create a somewhat separate presence for your professional or academic development. That's where pages can come in. Pages allow you connect with people without sharing your personal profile, and come with their own special considerations. Knowing how and why pages are used is the first step in leveraging Facebook for marketing yourself and your accomplishments.

CHAPTER FOUR

What Is a Page?

A Facebook page is a way for a business, organization, public figure, cause, or brand to share a public profile that can then be followed by fans. Whereas your personal profile can support a maximum of five thousand Facebook friends, a page can have an unlimited number of fans. And while your personal profile can be private, a page is always public.

WHY USE A PAGE?

You might wonder what the point of a page is when you already have a profile. Other than allowing you an unlimited number of followers, the features are pretty much the same as on your regular profile. You can post things that will appear in your followers' News Feeds, for example.

The answer is that a page lends an air of professionalism that your personal profile does not. On your personal profile, you'll likely want to post things that aren't necessarily relevant to your business or academic profile. If you have a separate page, you can keep that page entirely devoted to your résumé or portfolio. The people interested in your academic or professional development don't need to see pictures of you camping with your friends over the weekend—they're solely interested in your work and academic pursuits. By having a page, you can keep your professional life separate from your personal life. (For the most part, anyway— don't forget that nothing is *truly* private on Facebook, so you'll want to keep your personal profile fairly professional as well.)

If you have a portfolio of your work or achievements, a page is a great place to showcase them. You might have them on your personal profile as well, but be sure to put them on your page. If you're an artist looking to attend art school, you can create albums of your artwork and showcase them on your Facebook page. When you go about applying to art schools, you can include a link to your Facebook page so that admissions reps can take a look at your online portfolio. Because pages are always public, admissions reps will easily be able to see your best work when you showcase it on your page.

A page is also a great place to broadcast news about your profession. If you're an aspiring musician and you've landed a gig at a local club or event, you can create an event on your Facebook page and invite your fans to attend. People can even RSVP to your event, so you have a general idea of how many people to expect.

All of this can also be done on your personal profile, of course, but putting it on a dedicated page lends an air of professionalism and allows you to keep your private life relatively private.

So what are you waiting for? Let's create your page.

 ## NAME AND DESCRIBE YOUR PAGE

To create a page, go to Facebook, and in the Search field at the top of the screen, type "create a page" and hit Enter. This will take you to a page that lets you create a page based on your goal and content. There are six options: Local Business or Place; Company, Organization or Institution; Brand or Product; Artist, Band or Public Figure; Entertainment; and Cause or Community. Decide which one best fits your goal, and click on it. Each category will prompt you with one or more fields when you click on it—including the name you want for your page—and then you will click a Get Started button to proceed.

You'll be prompted to add an About description describing the content and goal of your page. Spend a few moments thinking about how you want followers to see your page—you want to make the goal of your page clear in your About section. Is your goal to keep fans updated about events you'll be

You can create one of six different types of pages when you set up your Facebook page.

appearing at? To have a dedicated space to share your art? Whatever the goal of your page is, make it clear in the About section.

Choose a unique Facebook web address to make it easy for people to find your page. Directing people to www.facebook.com/JohnSmithMusic is a lot easier than directing people to the generic, Facebook-assigned www.facebook.com/14758694, for example.

 ## UPLOAD YOUR PROFILE IMAGE

Just as you have a profile image for your personal profile, you'll have one for your Facebook page. You can either upload an image from your computer or import one from another website. If you choose the latter option, just be sure you have permission to use the image from another site. Your profile picture for your page should be something professional and appropriate that will reflect your page in a positive light.

 ## IDENTIFY YOUR AUDIENCE

When you create a Facebook page, you're given the opportunity to specify a preferred audience. Based on your specifications, Facebook will attempt to promote your page to your preferred audience. You can specify people in a certain geographic location; people in a certain age range; males, females, or both; people with certain interests; and people who speak certain languages.

If your goal is just to gain as many followers as possible, then obviously you'll keep your specifications really broad. But if your goal is to build a certain targeted small but strong audience of followers, you can get more specific. For example, if you're an aspiring rap performer, you might want to narrow your audience down to a specific age range. Although there are some senior citizens who are fans of rap music, they are likely to be few and far between, so it probably doesn't make sense to target them!

It's all about the audience. Who are the people who'll be looking at your page?

TELL YOUR FOLLOWERS ABOUT YOUR PAGE

Once you've created your page, you'll need to gain some followers. The first way to do this is to invite your friends to Like your page. When you go to your page on Facebook, you'll see a link on the left side that says "Invite friends to Like this page." If you click on that, you'll be able to select friends to invite to Like your page.

You can also use your personal profile to direct your friends to your page. If you post about your page, people in your Friends list will see the post, and they can follow it to Like your page. There can be a viral component to this, too—if you make your post about your page public, then when anyone Likes that post, it will appear in their friends' News Feeds: Jane Doe Liked a post on John Smith Music. Jane's friends who are interested in music might then click on John Smith Music to see what it's all about—and voila! More potential followers for you if they like what they see.

Don't forget to promote via other sources. If you created a custom Facebook web address, it's easy to promote your page by means other than Facebook. If you have a Twitter following, for example, you could tweet out a suggestion that people check out John Smith Music on Facebook. You could make that same suggestion in a caption of a photo on Instagram or Snapchat, too.

CREATE SOME CONTENT

For a page to be successful, you need content. You can create your own posts, just as you do on your personal profile, but you can also include links to other content your fans might find interesting. A good way to keep fans interested is to become the go-to repository for information. If you're an aspiring writer and your page is meant to be a portfolio of your writings, you can link to works other than yours that you've found inspiring or interesting. After all, people who like *your* writing are likely to also enjoy the types of writing that you like to read. You can drive traffic to your page if fans recognize that you are a good source for new information related to your field or area of interest.

Video blogs, or vlogs, are a popular type of content you can include on your Facebook page.

SCHEDULING POSTS

If you create a Facebook page, you want to ensure that it continually features new content to keep people interested. Add that content steadily—if you add five new posts at once and then nothing for a week, your posts are more likely to get lost. It's better to stagger those five new posts over several days if you know you're likely to be offline for a period of time.

You can do this by scheduling posts. In your page's Timeline, you create a post and then click the down arrow next to Publish. This will allow you to select Schedule, and then you can choose the date and time when you want the post to go live. This is a feature you *cannot* use from your personal profile. However, it is available from any pages you create.

LOOKING AHEAD

In essence, your Facebook page is like a website, only it's connected to Facebook. It's also probably easier to maintain than a website, and you don't have to pay any web-hosting fees! So make the most of it as a way to promote yourself and your interests or achievements.

Similar to a page, another useful Facebook feature is a group. Read on to find out how you can create and use a group.

CHAPTER FIVE

What Is a Group?

A group is a lot like a page in that it's dedicated to a particular interest. There are literally *millions* of groups on Facebook. Whatever interests you might have, or causes you might be devoed to, you can undoubtedly find a number of groups devoted to them. The difference between a group and a page, though, is that groups have a bit more privacy available. Pages are always public, but groups can be set to various privacy options.

CREATE A GROUP

To create a group, simply head over to Facebook and click the Groups link on the left side of the screen. That will take you to the Groups page. At the page's top-right corner you'll see a Create Group button, which can you can click on. You'll be prompted to create a name for your group, select a privacy setting, and add members from your Friends list. Once

PRIVATE VS. PUBLIC

When you create a Facebook group, you will automatically be the administrator of that group. As such, you will be able to change the privacy settings. There are three possibilities for group privacy: public, closed, or secret. You can also add more administrators if you choose, or you can be the sole administrator.

Public groups are, obviously, public. Anyone can join or be added to the group, and anyone can see what goes on in the group.

Closed groups are a bit more private. Members can ask to join or can be added by existing members. Anyone can see the group name and description, as well as who's in the group. But only members can view posts in the group and stories about the group on Facebook.

Secret is the most private option. New members have to be added or invited by an existing member, and only current or former members can see the group name and description, or find the group in a search. Only current members can who the group members are, as well as posts and stories about the group on Facebook.

If you're creating a group that you want to use to promote your business or academic profile, then chances are you'll want to make it public. Still, it's good to know about the variety of privacy options available for groups.

Is the content of your Facebook group a secret? If so, you can set options to protect your group's privacy.

you do that, your group will be created, and you'll be taken to its page.

 ## COMPLETE THE DESCRIPTION SECTION

When you arrive at your group's page, you can customize it by adding a description. On the right side of the screen, below the list of members in the group, you'll find a link to Add a Description. Click it to enter a description of your group.

Just as you did with your page, take a few moments to think about how you want to describe your group.

Your group might include just people you know, but more likely it will include a diverse set of people from around the world who happen to share a common interest.

What is the purpose of your group? What is its goal? You want your description to reflect exactly what you're trying to accomplish. If the goal of your group is networking with other artists in your genre, for example, say that in your description.

 ## UPLOAD YOUR GROUP IMAGE

A great way to customize your group is to choose a background image that reflects the group's personality. This image will be shown in the header at the top of the group. You can either upload a photo from your computer or choose a photo that already exists on your personal profile. As always, make sure that the image is appropriate and reflects the image you want to portray in your group. And if you're using an image that you didn't take, make sure you have permission to use it.

 ## INVITE FRIENDS TO JOIN YOUR GROUP

Your group won't be much of a group if it doesn't have any members. From your group page, just above where you entered the description, you can add members. Simply click in the box under Add Members, and you'll have the option to add members from your Friends list on your personal profile.

Depending on the privacy settings of your group, you can also promote it on Facebook or on other media. If your group privacy is set to secret, people won't be able to search for it—they'll have to be added by someone currently in the group. But if your group is set to public or closed, people will be able to search for it on Facebook and request to be added. In those cases, you could promote it by means other than Facebook, such as tweeting out the name of the group and encouraging people to join it.

 ## START A DISCUSSION

The success of groups depends on people actually participating in them. The best way to ensure this is to start interesting discussions within your group. Simply add a post to the group wall and encourage people to join in. Anyone who is a member of the group will receive a notification of the new post (unless they have turned off notifications from your group, which unfortunately you have no control over—that's up to each individual), and if you've posted an interesting, thought-provoking discussion topic, hopefully people will join in the conversation.

For example, if you want to get feedback on your latest piece of art, song composition, or short story, you could post it on the group wall and invite people to share their thoughts in the comments. Just be sure to put on your thick

skin in case you get any negative feedback—one downside to social media is that people sometimes feel free to be quite critical because they feel relatively anonymous. People are sometimes much freer with their negative opinions when they're not saying them straight to your face.

What will people be talking about in your group? You can use the description section to give members an idea of the group's main areas of focus.

Chances are your group is made up of people who like your work and are interested in it, so the vast majority of feedback you get will likely be either positive or constructive—not strictly negative and meant to be hurtful. Trolls exist on social media and will be negative just for the thrill of it, but if you find one in your group, you can always remove them. That's the beauty of being the group administrator!

LOOKING AHEAD

Now you understand personal profiles, pages, and groups, as well as the basics of how to use them all. Let's talk about some additional ways you can use Facebook to promote yourself or your business.

CHAPTER SIX

Activities to Keep You Going

Now that you better understand the power of Facebook beyond simply being a socializing tool, you can see how Facebook can be an excellent way to promote yourself to colleges or potential employers. Posting regular, relevant, targeted information will showcase your skills and talents and make you look appealing to both academic recruiters and potential employers.

A key word here is "regular." Post often enough that people don't forget about you, but not so often that your posts clutter up people's News Feeds. If you post too often, people may choose to hide your posts from their News Feeds, and you definitely don't want that! Post positive, useful information and post regularly, but not *too* often. Keep in mind these last few activities that can further help you present your résumé or portfolio.

Pictures are hugely popular on Facebook. Share images that capture the major moments in your life!

 ## POST PICTURES OR VIDEO

According to Facebook's Help Center, when you have a Facebook page, the posts that tend to receive high engagement from fans are photos and videos. People are visual creatures, and pictures and videos that are appealing to the eye will tend to draw viewers and comments. There's the old saying that a picture is worth a thousand words. It holds true on social media as well. Long blocks of text can be tedious to read, and

PICTURE PERFECT

Pictures are attention-grabbers, but the quality of pictures is not created equal. You've probably noticed that some of your Facebook friends consistently post eye-catching, crisp photos while others post any dark, grainy snapshot they take. If you're using Facebook to try to further your academic or professional profile, you'll want to ensure that the pictures you post are of the first type: clear, high-quality images.

The first and most obvious step is to take good pictures. Make sure that there's good lighting before you snap the photo and that the background isn't full of clutter, such as random people or objects.

If you've composed a good picture but you still want to clean it up a bit, try using an image editing application. Many people use their smartphones to take pictures to upload to social media now, and there are many useful apps that will help you quickly clean up your photos and give them a more professional pop. Photoshop Express Mobile, Photoshop Lightroom, Instagram (also a social media platform), and VSCO Camera are a few top-rated ones. They all work on multiple smartphone platforms.

fans will often scroll right past them or just skim them briefly. A picture or video provides your information in a quick view. Your fans are likely to spend the few moments it takes to study the picture or video and get your message.

Some interests lend themselves to this strategy better than others. For a musician, video clips of your live performances would be likely to draw interest from your followers. An artist can post good-quality pictures of work to promote themselves. But if you're a writer, you'll have to get a little more creative when you try to think about relevant photos or videos to post. If you do a reading at a local coffeehouse, post a picture of you at the event. Or perhaps a particular location or event inspired something you wrote. You can post a picture of those things as well. The possibilities for visual posts are there, even if you might have to think a little bit outside the box.

 ## CREATE OFFERS

The Facebook Help Center also reports that Facebook offers tend to earn a fair amount of interest from page followers. If you have a business page with at least fifty Likes, you can create an offer. Facebook allows you to customize your offer—you can tailor your offer to include any product or service, to whomever you want, in any particular quantity you want.

Offers will be more relevant for some interests than for others. Local musicians might offer one fan the chance to book a party at 50 percent off their normal rate, for example. An artist might offer portraits at a certain discount for a limited time. If your ultimate career goal is childcare and you're working to build up a babysitting business, you might offer discounted babysitting to a certain number of fans.

Creating an offer is free, but if you want to promote the offer there will be a fee attached. The fee depends on how you've created the ad—such as straight from your page or through Facebook's own ad-creation tool, called Power Editor—and how many people you want to promote it to.

Do you have a service or product to offer? You can create offers on Facebook, such as an offer for a discount on babysitting, if that's your business offering.

USE INSIGHT INFORMATION FOR DEMOGRAPHICS

If you have created a Facebook page and you have at least thirty followers who Like it, you can use Facebook Page Insights to determine audience demographics. You simply go to your page, click Insights at the top of the page, and then click People. Facebook will then show you a breakdown of the people who Like your page by age and gender. This is based on the informa-

If you are curious about who your fans are, Facebook allows you to determine the demographics of your followers.

tion people have entered on their personal profile, so obviously it depends a bit on whether people were honest in their profile. But most people are, so it's reasonably accurate. (One exception is minors—some parents will insist that a minor falsify his or her birth date to try to deter potential online predators.)

The Page Insights will also show you your followers' countries and cities. This information is quite accurate, as it's based on the IP address the person uses when they log on to Facebook, and that information is incredibly difficult to falsify. They'd have to be a master hacker to do so!

And finally, you'll see the primary languages of your followers, based on what they've set their default language as. Again, this is pretty accurate because people have little reason to choose a default language other than their primary spoken one!

 USE INSIGHT INFORMATION FOR ENGAGEMENT

You can also use Page Insights to find out various engagement data about individual posts on your page. The Posts section of your Page Insights will show you how many people your post reached, how many people clicked on your post, and how many people reacted to (generally Liked, although clicking on Love, Wow, Sad, Haha, and Angry counts, too), commented on, or shared your post.

You can use this information to tailor future posts. For example, if you find that you're getting the most engagement when you post photos, as opposed to text posts or video, you can concentrate primarily on that style of post.

 ## BOOST A POST

One feature of Facebook that annoys many people is the algorithms it uses to determine which posts are seen. If you've used Facebook to any extent, you've undoubtedly noticed that sometimes you miss posts that were posted hours or even days before. You might wonder *how* you missed them. The answer is Facebook algorithms. No one is immune to them—if you post from your page on Faccbook, your posts *will* sometimes get shuffled to the bottom of the News Feed, meaning that not everyone will see them.

To combat this, you can boost a post. This means you can ensure that your post appears higher up in people's News Feeds than it might otherwise. The downside is, this option is not free. The amount it costs depends simply on how many people you want your post to reach and for how long you want the post to be boosted.

On any post you make (new or previously published), you simply click Boost Post at the bottom of the post, and Facebook will allow you to choose the audience you want to reach and for how long, as well as set a maximum budget.

Obviously, boosting all your posts would be prohibitively expensive, so choose the posts you want to boost wisely. If you're going to spend money, make it work for you. Choose posts that you know will reflect your academic or professional goals in the most positive manner.

LOOKING AHEAD

Facebook is incredibly customizable. It's a useful tool when you're trying to create an online profile or portfolio that will enhance your chances of academic or professional success. Once you've worked through the activities in this book, explore more of what Facebook can do. Facebook's Help Center is incredibly comprehensive and detailed; it can give you many ideas for activities to promote your résumé or portfolio. There are countless blogs and news articles dedicated to working with Facebook that can provide you with more ideas.

However you choose to use Facebook, keep it professional and tasteful, and you will find it pays you back in positive responses. Good luck!

academic recruiter Someone who evaluates potential students who may be admitted to an institute of higher learning.

algorithm A set of rules used to calculate the solution to a problem.

brand A well-known identity or image.

content Information, especially information that is made available via an electronic medium.

cross-posting Sending the same message via multiple channels.

cyber predator Someone who uses the Internet or related technology to prey on a vulnerable person or group.

demographics Statistical data about a particular group.

engagement Something that sparks the interest of a viewer.

facial-recognition software Applications that can identify people in digital images by comparing patterns.

GPS Stands for Global Positioning System, a satellite navigation system.

infallible Incapable of being wrong.

IP address Stands for internet protocol address; a unique string of numbers that identifies the computer being used to communicate over the internet.

ironclad Impossible to weaken or break.

networking Connecting or interacting with others who have similar interests or goals.

portfolio A set of materials that displays a person's skills.

résumé A summary of education, experience, skills, and qualifications.

screenshot An image of what's shown on a computer or device screen.

social media Applications that allow users to share content with each other.

suggestive Of a sexual nature.

troll A person who seeks to generate conflict on the Internet by posting rude or inflammatory comments or content.

viral Related to a piece of content that is spread rapidly among viewers.

Boys & Girls Clubs of America
1275 Peachtree Street, NE
Atlanta, GA 30309
(404) 487-5700
Website: http://www.bgca.org/Pages/Contact.aspx
The Boys & Girls Clubs of America have different chapters throughout the United States, and many offer career and college readiness programs. Check out the main site to find a program near you.

Global Kids
137 East 25th Street, 2nd Floor
New York, NY 10010
(212) 226-0130
Website: http://www.globalkids.org
The nonprofit organization Global Kids offers college and career-readiness programs for young adults, both in schools and online. The group was founded in 1989 and incorporated in 1991.

OSCA/ACOSO
PO Box 60
Hillsburgh, ON N0B1Z0
Canada
(519) 800-0872
Website: https://www.osca.ca
The Ontario School Counsellors' Association (OSCA) offers career and education advice to students. The group's website offers entrepreneurship advice, self-assessment tools, career-planning tools, and information about apprenticeships and universities.

Pew Research Center
1615 L Street, NW, Suite 800
Washington, DC 20036
(202) 419-4300
Website: http://www.pewinternet.org/2013/05/21/
    teens-social-media-and-privacy/
This nonpartisan fact tank has conducted and pub-
    lished a number of studies on social media use,
    many of which can be found through its website.

Services for Youth
140 Promenade du Portage, Phase IV, 4D392,
Mail Drop 403
Gatineau QC K1A 0J9
Canada
Attn: Youth Operations Directorate
(800) 935-5555
Website: http://www.youth.gc.ca/eng
On its youth services website, the Canadian govern-
    ment offers a career planning website for young
    people in Canada.

United Way
701 N. Fairfax Street
Alexandria, VA 22314
(703) 836-7112
Website: https://www.unitedway.org/contact-us
The United Way has chapters throughout the United
    States, and many of them offer college and career
    planning programs. Check out the group's website
    to find one in your area.

YouthWorks Programs
401 Wood Street, Suite 1500
Pittsburgh, PA 15222
(412) 281-6629
Website: http://www.youthworksinc.org/for_youth/
    youthworksprograms/youthworksprograms.html
YouthWorks, located in Pennsylvania, sponsors career
    exploration programs for youths and young adults
    from ages twelve to twenty-five.

WEBSITES

Because of the changing nature of internet links, Rosen
Publishing has developed an online list of websites
related to the subject of this book. This site is updated
regularly. Please use this link to access the list:

http://www.rosenlinks.com/SMCB/face

FOR FURTHER READING

Abram, Carolyn. *Facebook for Dummies*. New York, NY: For Dummies, 2016.

Chritton, Susan. *Personal Branding for Dummies*. New York, NY: For Dummies, 2014.

Clark, Dorie. *Reinventing You: Define Your Brand, Imagine Your Future*. Brighton, MA: Harvard Business Review Press, 2013.

Cross, Matthew T. *The Resume Design Book*. Amazon Digital Services, 2016.

Fine, Robert. Editor. *The Big Book of Social Media: Case Studies, Stories, Perspectives*. Tulsa, OK: Yorkshire Publishing, 2010.

Johnson, Shelby. *Facebook for Beginners: Navigating the Social Network*. RAM Internet Media, 2012.

Kennedy, Grant. *Facebook: Master Facebook Marketing*. CreateSpace Independent Publishing Platform, 2016.

Marshall, Perry, Keith Krance, and Thomas Meloche. *Ultimate Guide to Facebook Advertising*. Second edition. Irvine, CA: Entrepreneur Press, 2015.

Ochs, Josh. *Light, Bright & Polite : How to Use Social Media to Impress Colleges & Future Employers*. MediaLeaders.com, 2015.

Richards, Michael. *Social Media : Dominating Strategies for Social Media Marketing with Twitter, Facebook, YouTube, LinkedIn, and Instagram*. Lulu.com, 2015.

Teens' Guide to College & Career Planning. Eleventh edition. Lincoln, NE: Peterson's, 2011.

Wolf, J. *Social Media: Master, Manipulate, and Dominate Social Media Marketing with Facebook, Twitter, YouTube, Instagram and LinkedIn*. CreateSpace Independent Publishing Platform, 2015.

BIBLIOGRAPHY

Ark, Casey. "14 Amazingly Free Stock Photo Websites." Entrepreneur.com. October 20, 2014. https://www .entrepreneur.com/article/238646.

"Beginners' Guide to Facebook." YouTube. April 22, 2013. https://www.youtube.com/watch?v =ewlC5p851KE.

Cassidy, John. "Me Media." The New Yorker. May 15, 2006. http://www.newyorker.com/magazine/2006/ 05/15/me-media.

Clay, Kelly. "Personal Branding Secrets From Social Media Superstars." Forbes Tech. January 21, 2014. http://www.forbes.com/sites/kellyclay/2014/01/21/ personal-branding-secrets-from-social-media -superstars/#6e1b68b01440.

Duggan, Maeve. "The Demographics of Social Media Users." Pew Research Center. August 19, 2015. http://www.pewinternet.org/2015/08/19/the -demographics-of-social-media-users/.

Emoult, Emeric. "How to Triple Your YouTube Video Views with Facebook." Social Media Examiner. November 26, 2012. http://www.socialmediaexaminer.com/how -to-triple-your-youtube-video-views-with-facebook/.

Hu, Elise. "Father: Teen Jailed for Facebook Comment Beaten Up Behind Bars." NPR.org. July 3, 2013. http://www.npr.org/blogs/alltechconsidered/ 2013/07/03/198129617/teen-jailed-for-facebook -comment-reportedly-beat-up-behind-bars.

"Learn How to Use Facebook Properly – Part 1." You-Tube. February 26, 2012. https://www.youtube.com/ watch?v=ZOAsc3Klb2Q.

Leland, Karen. "Personal Branding on Social Media." Lynda.com. March 7. 2016. https://www.lynda.com/

Facebook-tutorials/Personal-Branding-Social-Media/
417148-2.html.

Patrick, Maggy. "Internet Regrets Hit One in Five Amer-
icans Who Post on Social Media." ABC News. July
27, 2011. http://abcnews.go.com/Technology/internet
-regrets-social-media-users/story?id=14162983.

Pulido, Mary L. "Social Media Gone Awry: Tips for
Teens to Stay Safe." Huffington Post. May 22, 2013.
http://www.huffingtonpost.com/mary-l-pulido-phd/
social-media-gone-awry-ti_b_2923603.html.

"Social Media: Considerations and Implications in College Admission." National Association for College
Admission Counseling. http://www.nacacnet.org/
research/publicationsresources/marketplace/
documents/rptbrief_socialmedia.pdf.

"Social Media Presence and Admissions." IvyWise
Newsletter. https://www.ivywise.com/ivywise
-knowledgebase/newsletter/article/social-media
-presence-and-admissions/.

"Social Networking Safety." National Crime Prevention
Council. http://www.ncpc.org/topics/internet-safety/
social-networking-safety.

Teare, Chris. "Don't Let Social Media Hurt Your College or Career Start." Forbes Investing. October 18,
2015. http://www.forbes.com/sites/christeare/2015/
10/18/dont-let-social-media-hurt-your-college-or
-career-start/#4b0ebc026579.

Vahl, Andrea. "8 Ways to Use Faebook Video for More
Engagement." Social Media Examiner. February 9,
2015. http://www.socialmediaexaminer.com/use
-facebook-video-for-more-engagement/.

INDEX

A

academic recruiter, 17, 19,
    26, 45
algorithm, 52
audience, 33, 34, 50, 52

B

boost, 52
brand, 30, 32

C

code, 7
Contact and Basic Info, 23,
    26, 27
content, 4, 8, 13–15, 17, 19,
    22, 32, 36,
cross-posting, 9
cyber predator, 26, 27

D

demographics, 50
description, 32, 40, 41
Details About You, 23, 27, 28
discussion, 42

E

engagement, 46, 51, 52
event, 31, 32, 48

F

Facebook, 4,6–22, 24–33,
    35, 37, 38, 41, 42, 44–46,
    48, 50–53
Facebook Help Center, 46,
    48, 53
facial-recognition software,
    19
Family and Relationships,
    23, 27
followers, 30, 32, 34, 35, 48,
    50, 51
Friends Only, 16, 20

G

GPS, Global Positioning
    System, 27,
groups, 10, 12, 13, 37, 38,
    40, 41, 42, 44,

H

Harvard, 6, 7

I

image, 4, 14, 15, 19, 21, 25,
    33, 41,
infallible, 18,
Instagram, 35
internet, 6, 13, 14,

ABOUT THE AUTHOR

Cathleen Small is an author and technical editor living in the San Francisco Bay Area. She has written dozens of nonfiction books for children and young adults on topics ranging from technology to history to biography. When she's not writing or editing, Cathleen enjoys reading, traveling, and hanging out with her husband and two young sons.

PHOTO CREDITS

Cover wavebreakmedia/Shutterstock.com, monitor display Denys Prykhodov/Shutterstock.com; p. 3 everything possible/Shutterstock.com; pp. 4-5 background solarseven/Shutterstock.com; pp. 4-5 (inset) Image Source/Getty Images; p. 7 The Asahi Shimbun/Getty Images; p. 10 William Andrew/Moment/Getty Images; p. 12 Thomas Barwick/Iconica/Getty Images; p. 14 © iStockphoto.com/goldy; p. 16 Justin Paget/Corbis/Getty Images; p. 20 PYMCA/Universal Images Group/Getty Images; p. 22 Brendan O'Sullivan/Photolibrary/Getty Images; p. 24 Westend61/Getty Images; p. 28 Monkey Business Images/Shutterstock.com; p. 32 © iStockphoto.com/bombuscreative; p. 34 Pinkcandy/Shutterstock.com; p. 36 © iStockphoto.com/vgajic; p. 39 ColorBlind Images/The Image Bank/Getty Images; p. 40 Klaus Vedfelt/Digital Vision/Getty Images; pp. 42-43 Robert Daly/OJO Images/Getty Images; p. 46 Terry Vine/Blend Images/Getty Images; p. 49 Kevin Dodge/Corbis/Getty Images; p. 50 ra2studio/Shutterstock.com; interior pages checklist icon D Line/Shutterstock.com; back cover background photo Rawpixel.com/Shutterstock.com.

Designer: Michael Moy; Editor: Amelie Von Zumbusch; Photo Researcher: Karen Huang